ARE YOU READY FOR THIS ADVENTURE?

Written by E. Amber Finch
Created & Designed by
E. Amber Finch
Edited by Jazmine Keeton

The Adventures of Peeps:
Peeps Learns About Panama is dedicated to
Aunt Margie & Uncle Willy. Thank you for being
the owner of the coolest Silkie Chicken!
I appreciate your continued support while I write
this series of adventure books about Peeps.

Hi, This is Peeps the Silkie Chicken! Peeps enjoys learning facts about her new home.

Panama is a country in Central America.

It sits between Costa Rica and Columbia.

Now Peeps learned that the Panamanian landscape is made up of mountains, archipelagos, and coastal lowlands.

Mountains

Archipelagos

Coastal Lowlands

Peeps stood, overlooking a beautiful mountain view. The central spine of mountains and hills known as the Cordilleria Central, spans almost the entire length of Panama!

Peeps discovered that Panama is located between the Caribbean Sea and the Pacific Ocean. The Caribbean Sea is part of the Atlantic Ocean.

Atlantic Ocean

Caribbean Sea

Pacific Ocean

Oceans are very large bodies of water.

The Panama Canal joins the Caribbean Sea to the Pacific Ocean.

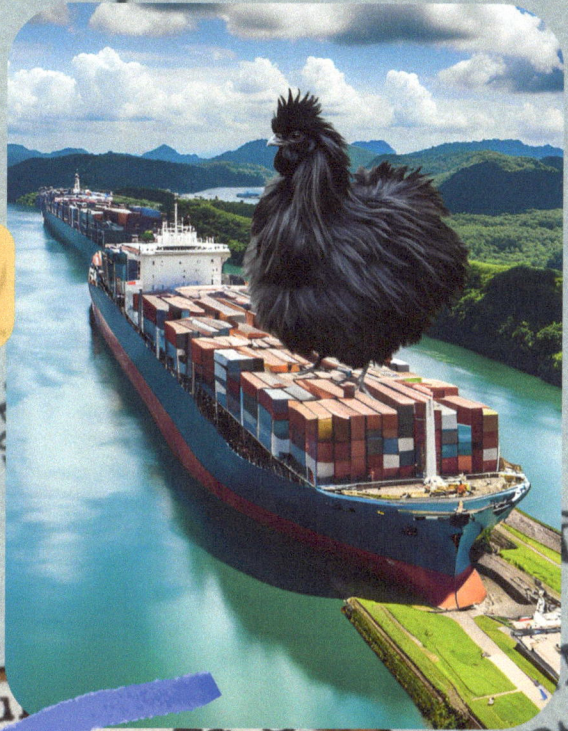

Peeps took a boat through the canal. Peeps watched the levies change during her voyage.

The national flower of Panama
is a white orchid called
the Flor del Espiritu Santo;
this means
Flower of the Holy Spirit.

Peeps loves flowers. What is your favorite flower?

Panama is a rain forest.
The Darién rainforest has a wide variety of animals.

Can you count all the animals?

Peeps counted ten animals! If you counted ten animals like Peeps that's awesome!

This is a Great Green Macaw! This parrot species is known for their beauty, intelligence, and charisma.

Peeps' tummy grumbled; it's time for lunch! Grace asked, "Peeps, would you join me and my friends for lunch?"

Absolutely! Let's Eat!

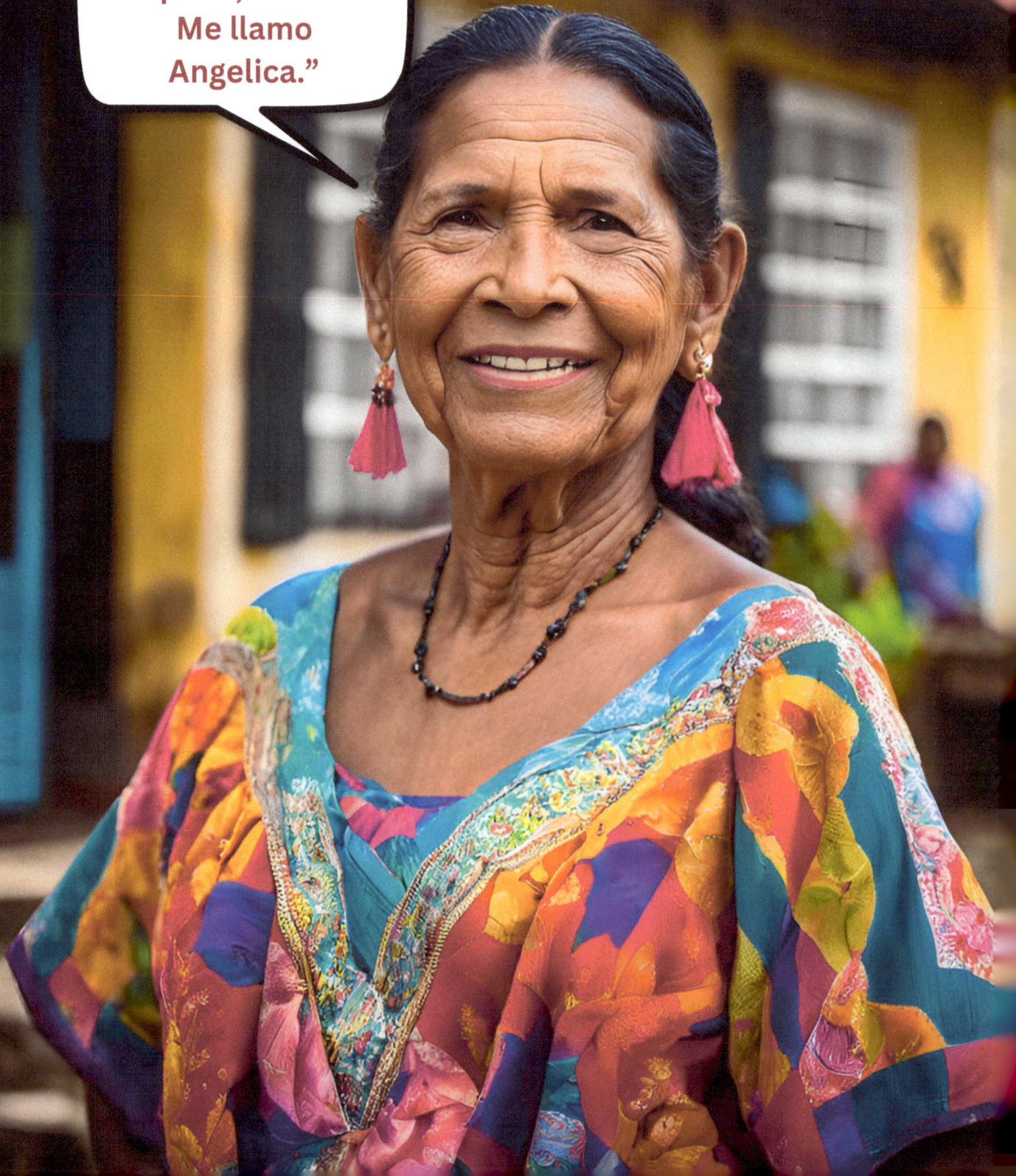

Peeps learned family is very important in Panama. Peeps met some new friends before lunch! Grace introduced Tootsie the Toucan. Lego's friend Maverick the white-faced capuchin told Peeps, "Lunch is ready!"

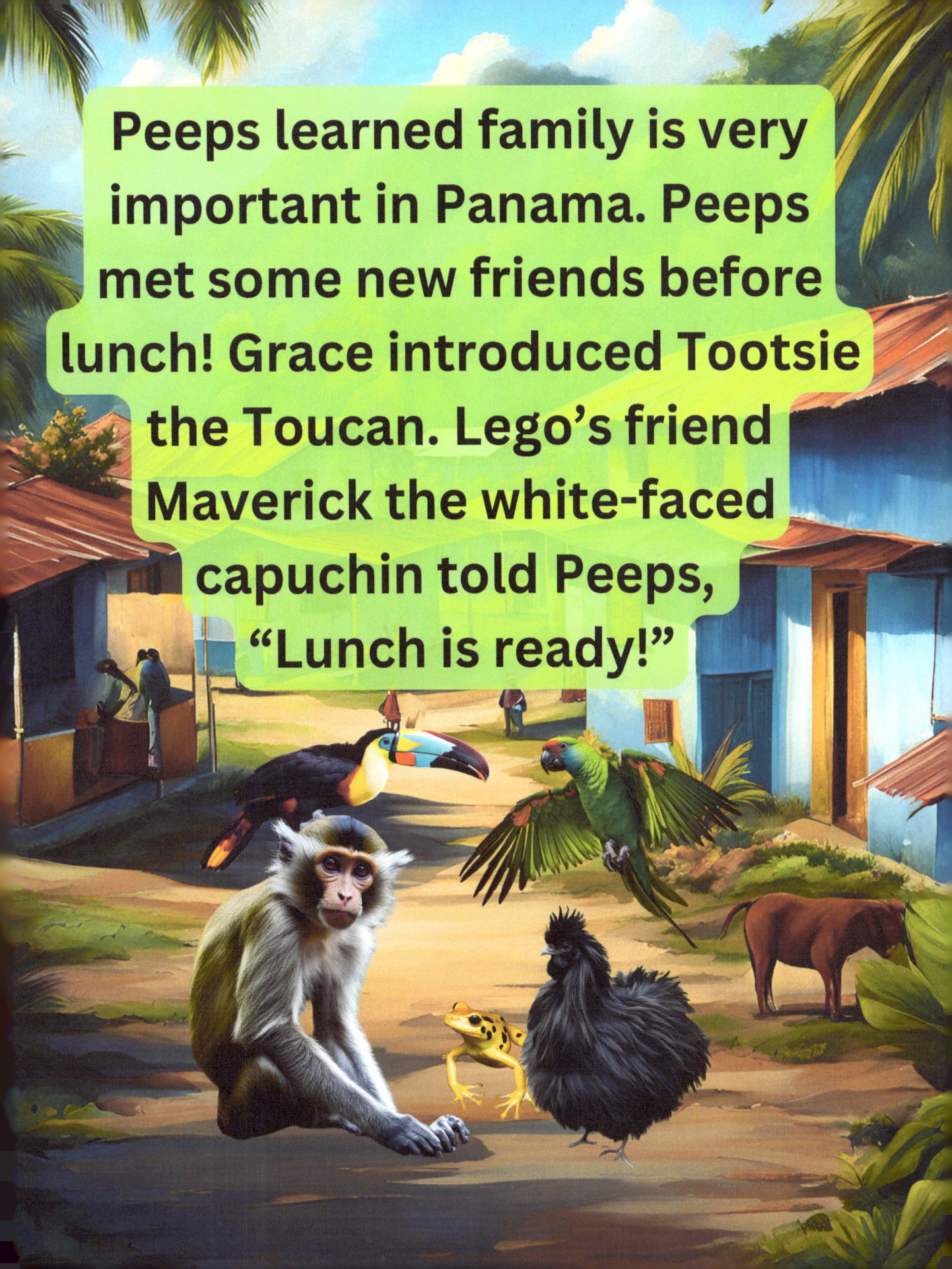

Peeps is excited to eat with her friends. Panamanians eat rice with most of their meals; they also eat corn tortillas with meat and vegetables.

Everyone agreed lunch was delicious!

Peeps enjoyed her new family of friends and all the fun facts about Panama! After eating the delicious food, Peeps decided on her next adventure!

Peeps is going to buy a farm!

Peeps is excited about her new adventure to learn how to farm! Do you like learning with Peeps? Read Peeps' next book!

The Adventures of Peeps
Peeps Learns How To Farm

JAMAICA

Caribbe

Sta
Marta

cigalpa

ARAGUA

L. de Nicaragua

Barranquilla

Cartagena

Monte

Colón

COSTA RICA

Puerto

Panamá

ntarenas

Limón

San José

PANAMA

Medellín

Manizales

Ibagu

Coco
(C.R.)

I. de Malpelo
(Col.)

Buenaventura

Cali

Popayán

Learn with Peeps:

1) What country did Peeps learn about?

Peeps learned about Panama.

2) What two oceans did Peeps learn that Panama falls between?

Peeps learned Panama is in between the Atlantic Ocean and the Pacific Ocean.

3) What two countries is Panama between?

Panama is between Coasta Rica and Columbia.

4) When Peeps took the boat ride what did she observe?

Peeps observed the levies.

5) How many friends did Peeps meet?

Peeps met 5 friends: Lego, Grace, Angelica, Tootsie, and Maverick.

ABOUT US ME

This is Margie, my husbands Aunt with Peeps in Boquete, Panama! Peeps is a REAL chicken who lived in Panama.

Thank you for reading The Adventures of Peeps: Peeps Learns About Panama written by E. Amber Finch.

Want more adventures with Peeps?

Peeps Goes To Panama

Peeps Learns How to Farm

Peeps Goes to Market

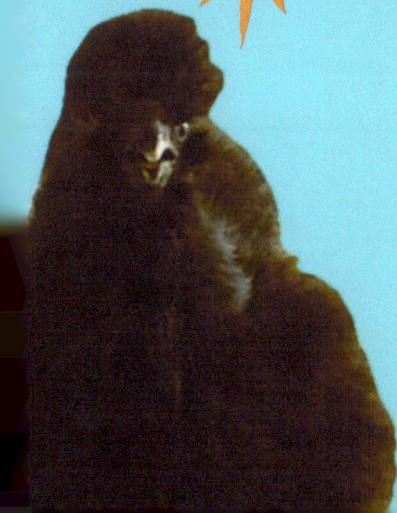

www.ingramcontent.com/pod-product-compliance
Lightning Source LLC
Chambersburg PA
CBHW042006100426

42736CB00038B/132